DATE DUE			

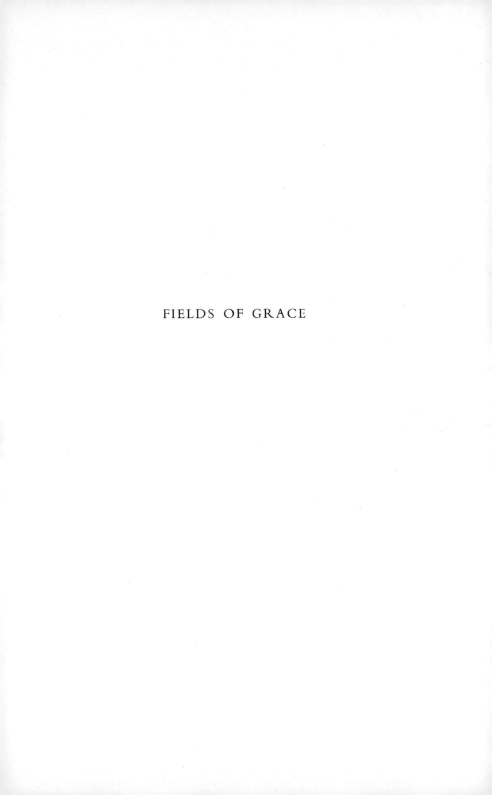

FIELDS OF GRACE

FIELDS OF GRACE

By

RICHARD EBERHART

NEW YORK
OXFORD UNIVERSITY PRESS
1972

ACKNOWLEDGMENTS

I am grateful to the Editors of the following publications
in which some of the poems in this book first appeared:
Antaeus; The Antioch Review; The Atlantic; The
Chicago Tribune; The Charles Street Journal; Concerning
Poetry; Genesis: Grasp; The London Times Literary
Supplement; Mill Mountain Review; The Nation; New
American Review; New England Galaxy; New York
Poetry; New York Quarterly; The New Republic;
Poetry; Poems from the Hills; The Quest; Quarterly
Review of Literature; Saturday Review; Shenandoah;
The South Florida Poetry Journal; The Southern Review;
Three Poems, 1968; The Virginia Quarterly Review.

The following poems first appeared in *The New Yorker:*
"As If You Had Never Been", "Despair", "The Fisher
Cat", "Homage to the North", "Suicide Note", "Track".

To
BETTY
DIKKON and STEPHANIE
GRETCHEN and ALEX

CONTENTS

THE YOUNG AND THE OLD

(For W.B. Yeats)

Will we make it to 2000?
1984 slides along ominously,
Now murder and assassination assail free Canada.
The center is not holding, Willie.
I sat beside you when the course was young.
I knew, old man, you would tell the truth.
How the young laugh at your singing Byzantium bird.
Ventriloquists all, no golden bough for them.
Who would want the intellect, that great stride,
Only to reach a tinsel bough. The drab
In the ditch is better, you thought of that,
The *Purgatory* knife the sharpest you ever honed.

We are easy riders to the fields of grace,
A bombshell in the gut.

No reality but in the spirit.

OLD QUESTION

I should walk maniacal
In the diabolical
But that reason should
Hold me to the good.

Why down in hell
Do men feel well
And why in madness
Know gladness?

We dare to tear
Ourselves apart
To know the true, the rare,
For the sake of art.

We are so in love
With life, that only death
Is strife
To be worthy of.

JOHN LEDYARD

Only death remains
To tell us
How great we were

Great with life,
The stone entablature
By the river

Tells us
Of a youth who made a canoe
From a cedar,

Descended the Connecticut,
Discovered far places,
Died the great voyager

Far from home,
Lost in Africa,
Youthful, valiant, destroyed.

That was in another century.
The incised bronze fades,
His name only remembered

By insignificant lovers in the Spring
Who read his story
And clasp each other,

Amazed at intrepidity
For all they want is themselves,
His valiancy hallucinatory,

His trial of the world incredible,
Their heroes themselves,
They only want to clasp each other.

Only death remains
To tell us
How great we were

Speaks the voice of the voyager
From fading bronze letters,
Great with desire.

VAN BLACK, AN OLD FARMER IN HIS DELL

Times of Archaic Splendour that you saw

There are times of archaic splendour that you saw
That when you saw them could not show
The unexaggeratable meaning of their drift
Which appeared in memory with unalterable flow.

You saw truth, you saw reality, the whole scene
Of man on the face of the earth, holding a rake,
And with muscles in his arms as big as baseballs
He pulled the gauze of summer to thick windrows.

It is his care that matters to us in the end,
His bent stance in the glaze of ancient sunlight,
The grueling work as if he had the mastery,
It is his lean tough luckless finicky endeavor

In the swift downfall of the year in August
Makes pathos grand, grand against granite cliffs
That tower above him inhuman, big as time,
Methodically he pulls on the rake's loose teeth,

Up on the cliff at the stealthy end of day
A buck leaps from rocks, held in sky light
An instant, so magical, so graceful, so final
He knows he has seen the glory of the world,

Will never be able to put in words this vision,
A throw of the eye beyond the field of raked nature,
A dazzle of the sense, archaic splendour of action
Lost forever: the buck leaping, the man gone underground.

FROTH

When the sea pours out under the bridge
Over the dam at every outgoing of the tide
There is ravishing serendipity of froth.
I stand on a hundred-year-old millstone.

Froth gathers on the turbulence of the waters
Abundant, fresh, puffed up. For hundreds of feet
Small cliffs, bluffs, towers form and seethe
From the turbulent center outward gliding,

Improbable as heaven, like a child's view of heaven.
How could anything so frail seem so permanent,
How could anything so sheer evade destruction,
These are things of imagination floating slowly away,

A white suds against blue water, white over blue,
A too much of nothing strangely become everything,
Froth dominating the presence of the world,
Cliffs, bluffs, towers and castles passing by.

It is good that everything has turned to froth,
Magical froth of truths going out to sea,
While I stand on the millstone solid and gray
I hear the airy shapes whispering infinity.

THE SWALLOWS RETURN

For five years the swallows did not build
In the treehouse near the door facing the sea.
I felt their absence as furtive and wordless.
They were put out of mind because they had to be.

Then they came again, two males attending one female,
Skimming in the late afternoon gracefully, ardent
And free in quick glides and arcs, catching flies on the wing,
Feeding their young in the house safely pent.

It was mid-summer, the time of high July,
Their return as mysterious as their former leaving.
They presented the spectacle of orderly nature,
Their lives to some deep purpose cleaving?

At night there was clamor. When morning came
The ground under the house was littered with feathers.
None knows who was the predator, but death
Is available to birds as to man in all weathers.

THE INCREDIBLE SPLENDOUR OF THE
MAGNIFICENT SCENE

When the seas are calm I cannot believe it,
The seas are so calm you would think
Passivity was the nature of man,

Yet you live in the illusion of the moment
When the seas happen to be indefinitely calm,
You live as if God had given you a grant.

God has given the grant and prize of peace
For this moment of calm on the sea before sunset,
God stays all the vessels from rolling and tossing,

Stays the mind from torment. Tales of misfortune,
The loss of vessels in storms, the death of seamen,
Tragedies of the sea of hundreds of years ago,

Comic misfortunes, hapless plight of victims,
Are erased before the quietude of the ocean,
Stay of every distrust, belief in the spirit,

For in beliefless calm of the ocean in August
Man hopes for the eradication of the intellect,
He hopes the calm of the sea will restore the heart,

He hopes he can say something true about mankind,
His empathy so pure he can find no word for it,
He sees the calm waters as a kind of benediction.

He sits by the shore and contemplates the waters
With reverence for the mastership of the universe,
Which is beyond and above comprehension.

This is a poem about the passivity of man
Because for a moment the ocean is passive,
The weather unalterable for an hour. Passivity

Suggests the dangerous activity of turbulence,
The mind comes again, the tug and sway of storm,
Antagonism returns, conflict, without resolution.

THE WEDDING

With a southwest wind blowing, late August,
Sally held a young seagull in her two hands.
With a love as supple as youth itself
In an ascending gesture she released the wild bird
In a moment of consummate grace and communion.

For an instant the girl and the bird were one.
Then the wild bird went to the wilderness of air
And the young girl returned to the confines of mankind.
Her gesture was like a release of the spirit
Held within the bounds of the corporeal.

Now we assemble on her wedding day
With no direct analogy in mind.
Bride and bridegroom here throw off the past,
But do they? Does a spirit of freedom hover
Over the future from the hand-held past?

TO KENYA TRIBESMEN, THE TURKANA

I love the Turkana tribesman who gave me his cane
Made into an eyelet of parti-colored wood, at Turkwell
On the Lodwar, southwest of Lake Rudolf, near Ethiopia.
I subscribe to the thin lips, the grace of the thin man.

I am beguiled by the stately grace of the young, barefoot girls,
Their naked feet held to the earth with moving cunning,
Each one Helen, immortal Helen, sweet Helens of Africa,
Tall, stately, naked, they were innocent of their glory.

The naked men with their spears seven feet tall,
The energy of tribesmen under the ancient trees,
Feathers arising from their heads, tattoos on their backs,
None old living, shining with tribal vitality.

What is this, old Death, how they have betrayed you,
I thought, incandescent creatures of an hour,
Here is no death, here is primitive lust, lust
For life, lust alive for thousands of years,

I am witnessing immortality,
They have no sense of a race with death,
Which is the surfeit of my Western poem,
They take me back to some immortal joy.

Boehme, Blake, Beddoes, be with me now,
You strove to know the truth of the real,
You would have loved to see the sights I saw,
Loved to know the feelings that I feel.

KINAESTHESIA

Sometimes I play the music of Charlie Byrd,
The dark rush of horses over the plain,
Confuse him with Charles Ives, fret of a flute,
The strings, the breath, and the interlocking time
Befit an inexpressible richness, lost unless
I try with poetry's imaginary gainsaying
To weave imaginable, placating harmonies,
Saving the mind for its penchant for newness,
While in the background are African Turkana shouts
Of the dance I saw under the thorn trees, ecstasy,
The brute mind of Beethoven breaking bonds
To say in the last quartets what I feel now,
An inexpressible richness, the austere, the sensuous conjoined.
Now the full fingers of Charlie Byrd play over the strings,
The austere face of Charles Ives strives from the record
Jacket, night flows under the heart in rivers of dream,
I am thrown along the decibels of the ages,
Music is the keys to the stars and the sea,
To the individual hour of the heart none shall forget,
Byrd and Ives joined, improbable, exquisite.

INABILITY TO DEPICT AN EAGLE

The eagles have practically left America.
Pouncing on an unexpected small creature,
Their talons fierce, they pick him to pieces.
Those great soaring wings that make us rejoice
Evantuate the male eagle to the top of a tall pine
From which he surveys illimitable ocean waters,
Flounces down on a lower abrasive nest; sated,
He reposes. He does not know that he has been poisoned.
Man the subtle, man the unknown, man the two-legged,
Has poisoned the food that feeds the bald eagles.

A psychic subtlety addresses the situation.
I have lost control of the bird as he has lost control
Of his subsistence. With an amazement bordering on devotion
I held before the movie lens the seven-foot wingspan
As the eagle took off and soared out over the ocean,
Made his powerful return to alight on the tallest pine,
Then drop to the rough nest. Alone. Was his mate killed
By the bullet of some ruthless American for sport?
Were his soarings looking for food, or for mate?
Is my self-consciousness more significant than his ignorance?

I held his heart in my telescopic lens with love,
I watched him in admiration in the tall summertime.
He was without equal. He was great in the skies in my eyes,
Only likened in majesty to some suffering poet
Who surveys the brutal headlands but is crushed to death
Almost before the realization of his scope,
Or like some voyager in the secrets of the soul
Who astounds us with the vitality of his presence
But who, like Socrates, is unknown in the market place,
Or like Christ, never tells us how it was on the Cross.

21

THE ANXIETY I FELT IN GUANAJUATO

The anxiety I felt in Guanajuato
In the second storey suite looking out
On the square to silhouetted theatre statues

Was a shaking and a reeling,
I saw a small boy leading a blind man
From the square down some ruinous street.

It was the blind man pulled by fate
My anxiety reached for. It acted
Like an incurable dictate.

The statues of the great actors,
Greater than life, were sublime
In their plaster indifference.

The small boy pulling the blind man
Put me into a frenzy of belief.
I watched, and did not move.

Deep down in the hilled cemetery
There are the corpses of Guanajuato,
Each held in his immortal gesture.

TRACK

Forced as I was, I ran a race with death.
I could not run a line as fine as his.
I ran it square, I ran it straight, but death
Was always out ahead of me, the winner.

As in a relay race, I strove to better time,
Hand on the baton with enthusiasm, spent
At the last instant, but adversaries ahead,
There were always adversaries ahead, cutting time thinner.

Now I walk as nature tells me to walk.
I like to think there is no competition.
I am myself. Whatever I am I am,
An end in itself. But death wants a new beginner.

He begins to loiter when I think. He slows
To notice and to savor my philosophy.
He cares for me too much, I think. God knows
What game he plays with me, Paraclete underpinner.

THE BOWER

Under dense fir boughs
On a carpet of pine needles
In golden summer afternoon
He came as to a cathedral
For the laying on of hands.

She came like the heart of summer
Beyond the reach of words
To exist in naked splendour
Where pain is forgotten,
To silent pleasure.

These two, realists of life,
Without a word to say,
Entered into the communion
Of old centuries, far places,
Zephyrs pleasing the sanctum.

It was a redemption as ancient
As lovers ever tried to imagine,
It was what battlefields are for,
To disclaim the evidence
Of the shooter and the shot.

They never thought of the suffering
Of the gross battlefield,
Under the serene pines
On a bed of pine needles
They never thought of wounds.

They never thought of useless death
Of boys killed in Vietnam,
Of the bloody passion
Of man to maim, to make blind,
The blood-drench of mankind.

They were in Eden, two
Enacting the high dream
Of purity beyond the evidence,
Their flesh effulgent
As in Rubens, Velasquez,

Zephyrs playing among the boughs
Nimble in the lightsome air,
Jets of purest silence,
Time suspended there
Looking on the timeless scene.

Lovers in their trance,
Death the deeper trance.
Dream of bliss, dream of death.
The strength of day wanes,
The blood of life pours out.

OUTGOING, INCOMING

My mind is that elusive thing,
An airy lightness, a superstructure of the air,
It seems more than air, darting
Flyer, having heft.

I cannot hold it in, I cannot let it out.
Hieroglyphs are written in the sky
If one but read. Fates they write,
The superstructures of mortality.

All that soaring, all that light
Plagues in nimble instances
The spirit to evade the flesh,
But birds fly back to grip the tree.

DESPAIR

O the snows last so long
And O man is such a brute
And O the girl is snatched by death
So fast you would not believe it,

And O I wanted to be tall,
And O the unendurable cold,
O that my mother was put away,
The long, the long trials,

And the love I had for one
It all went to pieces,
That girl who was murdered
And O that other my friend

Who set herself afire for nothing.
And O I hoped to be well
I wanted to be serene
O the snows last so long.

SUICIDE NOTE

I take no virtue of this as I finger the hand gun,
Insulted as I am by too much power of life,
Too small, too hurt in an alien place too large
To manage belief, victim of abominations.

Beyond the horror and the terror of the grave
I can make no moral distinction of good;
Evil overwhelmed me. I require
Obliteration and shall give it to myself

With one pull, impersonal, final, and timeless.
How to cross back through the vile tracks
That have brought me to this sane conviction
I am too depressed to know, too weak to care.

Veils and mists, mists, fogs and veils
Cover my life from the beginning to this end.
The tricky ways of the living were without help,
I go useless to the useless land of the dead.

It was the unrighteousness of the bad Germany
Without the hope of kindliness or mercy
Has brought me to the edge of the peace of my ruin.
I attest I cancel the letter you sent me, God.

MEDITATION OF GOD

If I were God I would be ashamed of being absolute.
I would absolutely want to be relative.
Warring man makes me see the truth of the relative.
I would be absolute, but absolute relatively.

Then I could leap into every heart
And there play an essential part,
I could penetrate into every man
And love him with my sole heart.

I could be true. I could be without reproach.
I could be kind to the undeserving,
Bless the evil doer and the murderer,
Claim as my own each selfish destroyer.

What I lack in Heaven is free will.
If I were free as is every man
I could admit evil as essential,
Praise the violent, evil, lust and pride,

Never supersede good and evil,
Revel as a devil and as an angel,
Raise Cain, and put down Abel,
Rejoice in lust, in the viable.

EVENING BIRD SONG

When the birds are singing in the bushes
They harp on evening.
I sing with them beyond disaster.
This generation does not know
The extermination camps of World War II.
This generation of birds does not know
One generation ago, its own generation.
How they inflate the exuberance of nature!
It is evening and all their song,
Pervading the pine trees in full summertime,
Reduces me to mindless ecstasy,
Increases me to nature's impersonality.

Nature careless of the human condition,
Hear the birds pour forth their vitality
In purity of existence beyond disaster.
They will be doing it a thousand years from now.
It is evening. Darkness comes. And bird song.

David sang, and lived, in part.

THE SOUL

The soul wanders in its own society
Displaced by birth, to be replaced by death.
It has no native habitat.

In the vast hungers of its loss
Maybe tides smothered in moonlight reap
A hint of the significance of sleep

And a bliss known in no actions of man
Come upon the eyelids when dreams come,
Maybe the deep is the truly real.

The soul that is time's wanderer
Cannot know the world's purpose
By war, nor save society, nor move

Men to perfect their ways and means,
The soul surrogate to the immeasurable.
In her deep waters mankind knows no sleep

Without the knowledge of the end of time,
It keeps what measures tend the absolute,
Drives through all, but knows not where to go.

Uproot man sees only a big chance
Which slides away in pregnant moons,
As he makes his loved mythology.

THE SECRET HEART

In the secret heart all men are free,
Each reaches for himself in his secret heart.
Try as we may for social harmony
Conflict strikes us in the morning,
Time takes us away in its mystery.

Night reveals the essence of our predicament.
Relinquishing consciousness, we sleep as dead
And arise to face eternal quandaries
Gripped by nature as was the first man,
Struggling like a medieval mendicant.

The status of power prevails for a while
But we sense in the health of our state
The sinister destroyer in the undiseased eye.
Eventually all ideas go underground,
The only triumph is some elegance of style.

To have lived a few decades virile
Is to have seen, say, in the city of New York
No sensitivity to the saving of monuments
But a race to destroy the historic part
As if the past were totally sterile.

Think, all living now will in time be dead.
Not a breather now who dreams on eternity
But will have it thrust on him early and surely.
We are compelled in this great adversity.
Some few will some great truth have said.

In the secret heart all are free,
Each has a secret heart of pure imagination.
Each man struggles with reality.
In the dark scales of birth who shall not say
That each man in his secret heart is free?

TIME PASSES

All is a kind of toys, all is a kind of play
In the great stack house of poetry.
Whether to say it out, or play it fey
Deposits truth upon society.

Which does not know which way it went
Until shufflings of many a fall
Settle the account of each event
And show at last that style is all.

The toys of the mind, the toys of the word
In high displays, in richest glows
Tell it better than it was
When the shifting heart would come and go,

So that society knows now
In the great stack house of poetry
The soul that shone upon the snow
And the eye of every pain.

BROKEN WING THEORY

The poet comes with his white pain to save mankind.
Few heed him. Necessity grips the neck and foot of each.
I see them pouring through the streets of years and decades
Bent on the tasks assigned them by necessity.

Most in words, most are wordless.
They do not think through, and if they thought
The spectre of death would arise to throw them down.
The poet comes with his broken wing to teach them flight.

THE LOOSENING

What loosens the eye?

   The sights of the world loosen the eye.

What loosens the ear?

   The songs of ancient dynasties.

What loosens the sense of smell?

   Dreams as deep as the breast of the mother.

What makes the tongue to taste?

   World so bright it talks in poetry.

What loosens the sense of touch?

   The sun arising, midday magnificence,
   Gorging floods of exulting blood,
   Wonder of time back to race infancy,
   Danger, and the danger of contemplation,
   Then space lost, the certainty of death.

There is a sense of something beyond us,
Uncapturable as the grace of a hummingbird,
Elusive as the death of a child you loved,
Shapeless as every final hope you had,
As mysterious as that you are still alive.

There is a glory that pertains to mountains,
To the seas, to man's dreams, ambiguities,
An ineluctable spirit in the nature of things
That makes us speechless before life and death
When we have suffered the limits of our consciousness.

THE FISHER CAT

Wildness sleeps upon the mountain
And then it wakes in an animal
And in us, and in the sophistication of city streets
And in the danger of the indifferent murder,
We see the fisher cat on the limb of the tree,
Or is it a marten, or what is this slim, fierce beast
Caught in the flashlight's glare at night in Vermont,
Ready to leap at the baying dogs?

This enemy, this ancient foe, what is he?
The unexpected beast glares down from the high branch
Ready to pounce and fills man with fear,
Some nameless fear of millions of years ago in the forest,
Or the Rift valley in East Africa
When it was life or death in an instant.

The man has a gun, the instrument that has saved him,
Without which the drama of this intense moment
Might have ended in the death of man, and no poem,
He raised his piece like a violator of nature
And aiming at the jeweled caskets of the eyes
Brought the treasure trove of brain and sport.

The beast fell to the ground, unable to comment,
His beauty despoiled that took millions of years to grow.
The dogs thrashed around a while and quieted.
The New England hunter then with his matter of fact,
Taking for granted his situation mastery, put the
Mythic beast in the back of his four wheel drive vehicle.

It has taken the scientists of the university months
To decide what kind of an animal the creature was.
The centimeters of the back molars were counted,
Books were consulted, in the end it was decided,
Not by the scientist but by the poet, that a god
Had descended on man, and had to be killed.
36

Wildness sleeps upon the mountain
And when it wakes in us
There is a perilous moment of stasis
When savagery meets equal savagery.
The long arm of man maintains intelligence
By death: his gun rang out instant doom.
The paws of the animal were very wide,
The claws of the beast were wide, long his thrashing tail.

READING ROOM, THE NEW YORK PUBLIC LIBRARY

In the reading room in the New York Public Library
All sorts of souls were bent over silence reading the past,
Or the present, or maybe it was the future, persons
Devoted to silence and the flowering of the imagination,
When all of a sudden I saw my love,
She was a faun with light steps and brilliant eye
And she came walking among the tables and rows of persons,

Straight from the forest to the center of New York,
And nobody noticed, or raised an eyelash.
These were fixed on imaginary splendours of the past,
Or of the present, or maybe of the future, maybe
Something as seductive as the aquiline nose
Of Eleanor of Aquitaine, or Cleopatra's wrist-locket in Egypt,
Or maybe they were thinking of Juliana of Norwich.

The people of this world pay no attention to the fauns
Whether of this world or of another, but there she was,
All gaudy pelt, and sleek, gracefully moving,
Her amber eye was bright among the porticoes,
Her delicate ears were raised to hear of love,
Her lips had the appearance of green grass
About to be trodden, and her shanks were smooth and sleek.

Everybody was in the splendor of his imagination,
Nobody paid any attention to this splendour
Appearing in the New York Public Library,
Their eyes were on China, India, Arabia, or the Balearics,
While my faun was walking among the tables and eyes
Inventing their world of life, invisible and light,
In silence and sweet temper, loving the world.

MEANINGLESS POEM

If I could write a poem without meaning,
To escape meaning altogether, to escape it,
For meaning ends in suffering. Oedipus,
Lear, Hamlet haunt me. I knew them young;
Now I know them still. They mean so much
Time does not lessen their meaning
But bears it harder to the heart as age increases.
As age increases the age decreases, time blurs
The focus hopes had on life's meaning.
The genius of man stated suffering.

The poem I would write without meaning
Would be the poem in the heart of every man
When he realizes his own obliteration, accepts
The senselessness of existence, knows he cannot
Stop the bird on the bough from singing, cannot
Know or control the destiny of his nation, himself,
Or of man; understands the disparities of reality
And of imagination; confronts the limits of will;
And as time forces him toward nescience,
Understands the indifference of the world.

But no, no poem can be written without meaning.
Words express a desire beyond suffering,
Worlds of religious significance suffusing
Illimitable reaches which we dimly perceive,
As when fog unwilled lifts, illuminating us.
It is a keen situation with our suffering
When we cannot accept suffering as totality.
The inner self sees a flash of eternity
As fog lifts, and knows in wordless immanence
Goat-footed gods splashing light.

ICICLE

It hangs down from the roof in a strict taper,
Formed by the violence of winter,
Dagger metaphor, its point to the earth.
Its life suggests against the earth increasing it.
It wanted to be ingrown as a contemplative poet.
Some rude sunlight would elongate it by inches,
Or, if unlucky, it would become dangerously long.
It objected to the gratuitous largess of nature,
It had been created as a reality of a season.
All life was seasonal, and all life would pass.
The icicle felt that it knew the human heart.
It waited patiently for time to destroy it.
Jehovah at first but elegant at last.

HOMAGE TO THE NORTH

After the swirling snowfall, days of whole
Downfall of individualized snowflakes' major patterns
When we work to keep up with the inches falling,
The world becomes a heavy lightness of light brightness,
One is given over to the softness of the December snowfall
As a foot or maybe an indeterminable two or three feet
Are swirling down from the heavens as time passes.
One feels the mass of it, wonders about danger
For man is rather quickly all too small a creature
Exulting in the primordial power of nature which may
Turn him to the opposite of his expectations,

And then the great cold like a clear white sting
Pervades the atmosphere as the snows cease to fall,
It is the power of the absolute god of winter.
We hover inside houses as night turns deadly cold
And awake to the awe and chance of thirty below zero.
Let man exult if he can, and he does, but narrowly,
We walk abroad in a kind of bravery of danger,
The invisible spectre of death visible before us,
Walking in cold that can kill, in our foot-salutes
To the white virtue, and in our heavy wraps
Clenching dictates from the god of the North.

AS IF YOU HAD NEVER BEEN

When I see your picture in its frame,
A strait jacket, pity rises in me,
And stronger than pity, revulsion.
   It is as if you had never been.

Nobody in the world can know your love,
You are strapped to the nothingness of ages,
Nobody can will you into life,
   It is as if you had never been.

I cannot break your anonymity,
The absolute has imprisoned you,
Most sentient, most prescient, most near.
   It is as if you had never been.

THE BREATHLESS

Something breathless hangs in the air
Of Gallinas Canyon, under the distant mountains
As if every dream of man suspended
Were as real unrealizable
As dreams realized in the here and now.

As that the brook is musical under Tres Alamos,
That the colt is elegant, in an absolute frisk,
That the Penitentes will never fail in their mission,
The spirit of the hermit is on Hermit's Peak,
That nature is ever a mystery to man.

If I could isolate a single quality
Of the perturbations and ravages of time,
Deny momently the forces of destruction
We inherit and shall not break, let me celebrate
A breathless quality in high mountain air. It is hope.

STEALTH AND SUBTLETIES OF GROWTH

I thought I could leave my habitation for the summer
Without the stealth and subtleties of growth
But when I returned to the summerhouse in Autumn
Vines and tendrils had shown their accumulated worth.

As if to say, you are dying, but we are living.
You go away to sea to champion new horizons,
Inveterate of lust, man of hope for the new.
You should have stayed home. We are your natural expression.

We have reached beyond the pruned and narrow.
We are the victorious life of vegetation.
We covered over the splendours of Angkor Wat,
We rode down the pyramids of Tehauntepec.

We may retreat from your tread and your private sickle,
It may seem as if you had commandeered our life,
Yet we, like you, look for the unwary principle,
March our fecundity as an absolute.

I almost heard the sermon of the tendrils
When I entered the airy summerhouse in September.
With deft expertise of strength of finger
I bent the vine, I broke it, and had some peace.

While you were away in the fields of imagination,
Cropping that hay, we have been gaining.
You may think you put us down with a finger
But we shall arise beyond your far dimension.

You are a twin of nature, but time will lop you
After millennia. You tried to conquer nature.
Too much intellect begat your downfall
In wastes of space. We do not outdo ourselves.

I saw the voiceless tenacity of green shoots
Overwhelming the earth by rigor of law,
Then laying an admonishing finger to a tendril
Murmured, "I live, you have no imagination."

EMILY DICKINSON

He saw a laughing girl
And she said to him
I must take a man
Toward eternity.

Her flesh was soft and fleet,
Her mouth was like a pose,
And a spiritual drift
Played about her flowing clothes.

She said she could not be
An evidence of the free
Unless she left her body
To become immortality.

She took him in the main
And held him in a trance
Who never knew for thirty years
Whether she was the dancer or the dance.

II

She was the highest mark
To which he set a snare.
He held her in his clutch
But she vanished in the air.

She departed with the years
And rode upon her destiny
While he was retained much
In the hold of mystery.

Now he must forswear
The roil of reality
And must admit the truth
Of what he cannot see.

She is gone with the wind
And he is gone with the weather.
Only in spirituality
Can they be said to be together.

Pretend to the flesh,
But the flesh will fall away.
In timeless uselessness
Love can have a stay.

He thought he held her
When passion was high.
Time brings her to him
In a long, in a wind-drawn sigh.

HARDY PERENNIAL

In youth we dream of death,
In age we dream of life.

> I could not have cared less for life
> When young, employing savage pursuit
> Into the glories of the unknown,
> Fascinated by death's kingdom.

> The paradox was my brimming blood.
> My bright, my brimming blood, my force
> And power like a bridge to the future,
> Could not contain itself in white flesh.

In youth we dream of death,
In age we dream of life.

> Now that death's savagery appears,
> Each day nipping at my generation,
> The hard facts of the world negate
> Symbols of the mind striving otherwhere.

> I would give love to every being alive,
> Penetrating the secrets of the living,
> Discovering subtleties and profundities in
> Any slightest gesture, or delicate glance.

WHERE I WANT TO GO

I want to go into the land of excess
Where the heightened awareness of truth
Defeats the negative specialists
Who run the world, scientific absolutists.

Excess leads to the realm of joy,
Joy is what all children know.
It is the joy of the heart I acclaim,
It is the joy of the sky that I feel.

I would be so in the miraculous
That I could tell a secret sure
That every man of imagination
Could be a child, be as pure.

It is a bright leap into air
To hold life holy there
And it is a bright leap of man
To leap into reality in the air.

ABSOLUTE SILENCE

Is an event in time to be wished.
It is an absolute,
Is clean, is final,
Our life before our birth,

Our life after our death.
Freedom of the age,
So vast it has no geography.
The freedom of the ear from hearing,

As if angels were playing.
And no taste of the world,
No touch of the tongue to flesh,
No incrimination, no anguish,

But like the blessing of innocence
After the fury of knowledge,
Like the sense of the court
Before a final judgment,

Something so deep it is wordless,
In prison the long thoughts,
In love bliss,
In death negation.

EMERGING

Bespeak the silence
Of lowest winds along the shore,
It will come in strength
When winds are no more.

Bespeak the strong gestures
Of the child who cannot speak.
His efforts rend the heart
As O how high his eyes seek.

What is that sound along the shore,
And what is that silence brimming?
Is it not suffering living,
And art again beginning?

Say nothing to the mystery
That is always emerging
From time's old clutch,
The birth of meaning and being.

THE PRESENTATION

I sense the purity of the Spring snowstorm.
The April flowers close up their eyes
As whiteness purifies the old encrustations,
Tabby, black and white, neighbor cat,
Strolls across the street purely occupied.
She takes time as a matter of course.

Wet heat of Yucatan, dry cold of New Hampshire,
Majesty the word for Uxmal and Chichen-Itza,
Mystery the term for the vital Indians
Who built stone on stone conceptual ruins
Whose paganism defied the Spanish conquest,
Compelling in style still, stone on carved stone.

What will we leave but twist and rust of girders
Centuries hence for the concentrations of New York?
What will we have handed down to survivors,
If wit sheer off self-annihilation,
To compare with ritual art of the Mayans?
What secrets will we leave they have on stone?

Tabby admirable, silent symbol black and white,
She will walk by flowers closed or open.
Whether the world is white, or if new green,
She does not know whether she is black or white.
I saw the emerald-eyed stone jaguar
Sixty fetid steps up, timeless in a Mayan temple.

What jungle flesh, what deaths, what triumph
Brought the imagination to so firm a state
In that hot vault, deep in a pyramid,
High up in the center, near the apex,
What but the baleful presence of the real,
Death and life in the power of a crystal eye.

IDLENESS

The spectacular apprehension of reality
　　As it were a biff, and a lance, and an eagle,
　　　　Brought him to the girl in the grass.
　　　　It posed the problem of reality.

Is love a prefiguration of essences,
　　The lady grasp of knotty simulacra,
　　　　The old, Emersonian, closed Over-Soul,
　　　　Or is it the bravura of a cheek?

Is it the wishes you have made,
　　A lash to undo death itself,
　　　　The lovely, lacy, wildflower longing,
　　　　Or is it the bowsprit flesh's gift?

What is love? Mortal, or shy immortal?
　　Is it ultimately a daring,
　　　　Is it the present senses' touch,
　　　　The reach of the lute, ten-fingered recorder?

Is it the configuration of the sea,
　　The osprey's egg's shell, white, spied,
　　　　Is it a violence, a tenderness,
　　　　The unknown quality of the air?

Is it, perhaps, the rich singing being
　　Of the supple feeling of invention,
　　　　Is it the unstated rinse of the sea's haul,
　　　　The darkest sleight, a mermaid tendency?

I have noticed, in the airs of summer,
　　A golden counterpart, the grassy lurch,
　　　　I have wondered on the void stars
　　　　And have held to the world, its plunder.

Where is reality, or the truth-look —
    In some distant rarity, sublime,
        Or is it in the unconformable truth
        In the decorations of the earth?

Is it a bible I read in the grass,
    Old, suffering lament of the ages,
        Or sprightly knowledge at the finger-tips,
        A light bloom of summer on the tongue?

Girls in grasses heavenly sweet
    Who seem to tell us what we are
        Are symbols of love in the mind
        And symbols of the spirit's reach.

QUARREL WITH A CLOUD

You rise like a mountain over the white building.
You are white, surrounded by blue.
You change me as I change you.

My quarrel is insurmountable.
You alter the landscape and change
Your being even while I am looking.

I have to think that I change you,
Being a man of will, but you
Do not know what you are doing to me.

It is an ancient dialogue
Of the inner and the outer world. I
Cannot, after all, contain you.

Already you have soaked up color,
Blushing rose; amorphous cloud,
You are undoing yourself among high airs.

The white building seems little changed.
You are vanishing in the heavens
And I am struggling with the word.

If I could fix you on a page
It would be an arbitrary election.
Clouds come and go. So do poems

In their world of white, and blue,
And rose, a make of the world,
Apparent, yet unable not to change.

Now I lay down my quarrel
In the heart of the word, rejoicing
In the nature of visionary change.

GNAT ON MY PAPER

He has two antennae,
They search back and forth,
Left and right, up and down.

He has four feet,
He is exploring what I write now.

This is a living being,
Is this a living poem?

His life is a quarter of an inch.
I could crack him any moment now.

Now I see he had two more feet,
Almost too delicate to examine.

He is still sitting on this paper,
An inch away from An.

Does he know who I am,
Does he know the importance of man?

He does not know or sense me,
His antennae are still sensing.

I wonder if he knows it is June,
The world in its sensual height?

How absurd to think
That he never thought of Plato.

He is satisfied to sit on this paper,
For some reason he has not flown away.

Small creature, gnat on my paper,
Too slight to be given a thought,

I salute you as the evanescent,
I play with you in my depth.

What, still here? Still evanescent?
You are my truth, that vanishes.

Now I put down this paper,
He has flown into the infinite.
He could not say it.

THE TRUNCATED BIRD

He stepped out of bed at night.
He turned on the light. In the blur
Of the first, stupefying sight
The upper half of a scarlet tanager

Lay on the rug. The severed bird
Lay like a comic mask, dropped
By the cat in the night unheard.
For a moment everything stopped.

Equal to supposing life whole
He lived in a forceful equipoise.
Some say this was the soul
Burgeoning while it subtly destroys.

MAN'S TYPE

When he considered his linguistic fallacy
He was thrown back to the primitive subhuman,
In consternation at the rise of man,
English not lasting millennially.

Something attractive in that slight figure
In the Rift valley millions of years ago,
Slinging his weight, craft outwitting his prey.
The crudest action would be long to stay.

Deft we are still to maim and kill,
We have the big means, the lack of sensitivity,
The annihilating energy.
Of redeeming grace who shall say?

LENSES

I

You go over the water from mooring
Hundreds of times in some years.
You cannot see the bottom.

I caught the ocean lens-like once,
It happens seldom,
Still, no ripple, direct sun

Revealing a clear underworld.
There was a ledge far down,
A long line of rock.

Off the rock a deeper tone
Showed mysterious depth
Remote and intangible.

I stared into that depth
Unable to see its depth,
Not knowing the end of it.

I knew how we go accustomed ways
Riding on the surfaces of time,
Not knowing the depth of our being.

We cannot live there,
Ripples come over occluding the view,
We point our motor to the shore.

II

O my boyhood, so religious, so affirmed
By every thing in nature that I saw,
The earth sumptuous, the new hay

We cut under the cedar trees
And carted off in happy haze of sweat;
The orchard trees, with gauze of blossom,
Later the rich apples falling to the ground;
Later still, the sweet scent of the cider mill,
With bees in burn of day to sip the liquor;
The time of running on the meadow;
The old swimming hole down by the Cedar river,
Where is this lost paradise of earth,
Lost in the center of the mind far back,
Obscure, illimitable, where?

Where is the order, harmony, and purpose,
The sense of love we had in the real?

III

I left the mooring, the motor purring,
To make another trial of finding.
I went far out in deep water,
As far as to an island shore,
Paying out the umbilical road.
I looked upward and saw an eagle,
Rarest sight, flying off a treetop
Beating my sight with definition,
The powerful beating of his wings
As he climbed, and soared, and climbed
Lost to sight soon miles away.
He left a vacancy in the mind,
A loss, an eagle-emptiness,
The whole vast heavens neutral, vague.
I departed from that shore,
Pulling up the heavy, fifty-pound anchor.

61

IV

Since when, many events, estates and trials.
Of earth, water and air I knew.
I knew of intellectual fire,
Fires of hell, hells of fire.
As a boy I used to fan
A small fire under a bush
Which grew up so bright and clear
I kindled by it, then plowed it under.
I sense going out down time
And if a hell of fire, a fire of hell
May be the end of time,
Ash strewn on waters under clear sky,
Ask our words to say
What deep void then shall we know?
What is deeper that nothingness?
The anchor we use is a plow.

LONG TERM SUFFERING

There will be no examination in Long Term Suffering,
The course will come to an end as planned.
I have found that examinations are useless,
We have altogether too short a time to spend.

Time, ladies and gentlemen, is the great examiner.
I have discovered that this is true.
It is what you write as you go through the course
Is the only determinant and determinator of you.

Long Term Suffering is for those of all ages
In our tussling University, our bulging classroom.
It may be that I will profess near madness,
It may be that you will write out your doom.

All that you will have at the end of the course
Is writings you indite, or poems you make,
If you make them. Words, words in a sea flow;
At any rate, a lot of heartbreak.

Save your papers. It may be that years later,
Forty, maybe, you would like to look back
At your course in Long Term Suffering,
And note how strangely you had to act.

YOU THINK THEY ARE PERMANENT
BUT THEY PASS

You think they are permanent but they pass
And only contemplation serves to save their memory.
You are in the Pan-World building with the leaders.
They all seem real, they all seem permanent

But soon you are in the Pan-World building with the past.
How closely and with what immediacy
You scrutinize the features of each noted face,
President, old poet, Supreme Court chief justice,

Secretary to the United Nations,
How lively their speech, lively their looks,
As all together in one banquet place
You would think there would be no end to this.

Who in the reality of his high days
Thinks of the destitutions of the night?
You think they are permanent but they pass
To feed ravens of the ravenous past.